The Best of Mary M
Barnyard

Back View
of Barn

mary maxim

Mary Maxim, Inc. 2001 Holland Ave., Port Huron, MI 48060 • www.marymaxim.com
Mary Maxim, LLC. 75 Scott Ave., Paris, ON N3L 3G5 • www.marymaxim.ca

LEISURE ARTS, INC. • Maumelle, Arkansas

Barn Yard

SHOPPING LIST

- ☐ Worsted weight yarn (refer to master key below)
- ☐ Tapestry Needle #18
- ☐ 8- 3" Plastic Canvas Circles
- ☐ 7- Clear 7 Mesh Ultra Stiff Plastic Canvas 13.5" x 22"
- ☐ 7- Clear 7 Mesh Plastic Canvas 11" x 14"
- ☐ 5- Beige 7 Mesh Plastic Canvas 11" x 14"
- ☐ Small amount of stuffing

SIZE:

15" x 11" x 13" [38 x 28 x 33 cm]

Please read all instructions included on page 42 before beginning.

INSTRUCTIONS:

This project has a lot of pieces and several are very similar. You may want to cut out just the pieces you'll be working according to the instructions.

Refer to layout diagrams (pgs. 6-8) to fit pieces as needed on plastic canvas sheets.

INTERIOR BARN

1. Cut out all pieces from pages 9-20 and 22-23 from the indicated canvas. Set aside the pieces for the animal pens. All beige canvas is unworked.

2. Center the front support piece on the interior front piece.

3. Using medium tan, join these pieces together along the indicated rows near outer edges and around the door opening. The right side of stitches should be on the beige side.

4. Repeat with back support and the interior back piece.

5. Join the side support pieces to the left interior and the right interior side pieces along the indicated rows.

6. Attach the base support piece to the interior base along joining rows.

7. Using medium tan, join the interior front, interior back, left interior side and right interior side at the corners to form the barn's interior, with beige canvas on the inside.

8. Join the barn interior to the interior base.

9. Using medium tan, attach a small pen piece to each joining row on the interior front and interior back from A to B.

10. Join the left divider to the center joining row of the long pen piece.

11. Join the front left gate and the back right gate to the long pen piece, matching the letters.

12. Tack the bottom of the long pen and left divider to the interior base at the X's.

13. Join the left divider to the left interior side wall as indicated.

14. Attach a right divider piece to the joining row on the sheep pen front piece.

15. Join the other right divider piece to the joining row on the pig pen front piece.

16. Join the center gate and the front right gate to the sheep pen front piece, matching letters.

17. Join the back left gate piece to the pig pen front piece from K to L.

18. Tack the bottom of the sheep pen front and the pig pen front and their right divider pieces to the interior base at the X's.

19. Join both right divider pieces to the right interior side wall along the joining rows.

Master Key

- / Red - 240 yds.
- / Natural - 120 yds.
- / Lt. Grey - 104 yds.
- / Med. Grey - 94 yds.
- / Black - 56 yds.
- ◇ Lt. Tan - 76 yds.
- / Med. Tan - 60 yds.
- / Brown - 26 yds.
- / White - 36 yds.
- / Peach - 26 yds.
- / Lt. Blue - 6 yds.
- / Med. Blue - 24 yds.
- — Joining Lines

20. Pass a piece of medium tan yarn through the O on the pig pen front piece. Form a loop about 1" long that will slip loosely over the top end of the center gate piece to "keep the animals in the pen". Tie a knot and trim ends.

21. Repeat at the O on each of the small pen pieces.

22. Cut the pieces as shown on pgs. 21 and 24 from large canvas sheets.

23. Using light grey, attach a lower roof support piece to each interior lower roof piece along the joining rows.

24. Attach a top roof support piece to each interior top roof piece along the joining rows.

25. Join an interior top roof piece to each interior lower roof piece from A to B.

26. Using medium tan, join an interior lower roof piece to each interior side piece between the triangles.

27. Using light grey, join the interior top roof pieces together from C to D.

28. Using medium tan, join the interior roof pieces to the interior front and interior back pieces.

EXTERIOR BARN

1. Cut out and work the exterior front (pg. 25), back (pg. 26) and side pieces (pg. 27) as indicated.

2. Using red, overcast the top edges of the front and back between the triangles.

3. Using natural, work the long stitches on each window.

4. Cut out and work four small door pieces (pg. 25). Overcast all edges of each piece with natural.

5. Tack two doors to the exterior front and two to the exterior back at the O's.

6. Cut out and work four medium doors (pg. 26). Do not work the small medium grey stitches that go over the edge of the canvas at this time.

7. Using medium grey, work the long stitch hinges as indicated on two of these doors.

8. Using natural, join a medium door with hinges to a medium door without hinges along the long unhinged edge.

9. Repeat to join the other two medium doors.

10. Using natural, cut out and work the stitches on one of the shorter door latch pieces (pg. 27) and overcast all edges of this piece.

11. Gently bend this piece into a slight curve and tack its short ends to the door (with hinges on the right side) at the joining marks.

12. Hold two of the longer door latch pieces together with all edges even. Use natural to join these pieces by overcasting all edges and then tack it to the other door (hinges at left) as indicated. The untacked end of this piece should extend over the edge of the door.

13. Using natural, join the other three edges of each door.

14. Attach the medium doors to the exterior front piece by working

the medium grey stitches at edge of hinges as indicated.

15. Repeat to cut out, stitch, assemble and attach the large doors (pg. 28) and their latch (pg. 27) to the exterior back piece.

16. Cut out two exterior top roof pieces and two exterior lower roof pieces (page 29).

17. Work the medium grey stitches on each piece and fill in with light grey half cross stitch. Do not work the joining row on the exterior lower roof pieces.

18. Using natural, overcast the lower edge of the exterior roof pieces between the triangles.

19. Using medium grey, join an exterior top roof piece to the upper edge of each exterior lower roof piece, matching at A's and B's.

20. Using light grey and medium grey to continue the roof pattern, join the top edge of one exterior side piece to the wrong side of an exterior lower roof piece along the unworked row. Repeat to join the other lower roof piece to the other exterior side piece.

21. Using natural, join the exterior front and back to the exterior side pieces at the corners.

22. Using medium grey, join the exterior top roof pieces together.

23. Using light grey, tack the roof to the exterior front and exterior back pieces.

24. Cut out and work the lower and upper roof trim pieces (pg. 28).

25. Join two upper roof trim pieces together from A to B. Join a lower roof trim piece to the upper trim from C to D and from E to F. Overcast the long straight edge of this assembly.

26. Repeat to assemble (and overcast) the other four roof trim pieces.

27. Using natural, join the unworked edges of a roof trim assembly to the edges of the exterior roof pieces.

28. Join the other roof trim assembly to the other end of the roof.

29. Using natural, tack the roof trim to the exterior front and exterior back pieces.

BARN ASSEMBLY
1. Slide the exterior barn over the interior barn.

2. Using red, join the interior and exterior pieces along the sides and top of the door openings.

3. Cut out the exterior base piece (pg. 30) and set in place and use red to join it to the exterior front, exterior back and exterior side pieces.

4. Using medium tan, join the interior base to the exterior base at both door openings and overcast the unworked edges of the exterior base.

FENCE
1. Cut 16 fence pieces and 8 fence bases (pg. 31).

2. Holding two fence pieces together with all edges even, use natural to join these pieces together by overcasting all of their edges except the bottom of the middle fence post from Y to Y.

3. Work the overcasting from Y to Y on each piece separately.

4. Using light tan, work the fence bases in half cross stitch and overcast all edges of each piece.

5. Using natural, tack the bottom edges of a fence piece to a fence base at the X's.

6. Spread out the bottom of the middle fence post to tack it in place.

ANIMALS
1. Cut out the pig sides, bellies and bases (pg. 31).

2. Using light tan, work the bases in half cross stitch and overcast the edges.

3. Work the sides and bellies in peach half cross stitch. Do not work the joining rows.

4. Divide a length of brown into individual plies and use 2 plies to work the long stitches on each pig piece. Make French knot eyes by wrapping the yarn around the needle only once.

5. Using peach, join a pig belly to a pig side piece from A to C. Join this same belly to another pig side piece (facing the other way) from D to E.

6. Join the belly to the pig from E to F and from A to F.

7. Continue joining around the head and body, inserting a small amount of stuffing as you work.

8. Join the belly to the pig from C to B and D to B.

9. Overcast all edges of the legs and tack them to a pig base at the X's.

10. Repeat to make 2 more pigs.

11. Cut out all sheep and goat pieces (pg. 32) and 2 goat bases (pg. 33).

12. Using light tan, work all bases in half cross stitch and overcast all edges.

13. Work the half cross stitches on all sheep and goat pieces. Three sheep will be done in white and one in black. One goat will be done in light grey and one in medium grey.

14. Using light tan, work the 4 stitches at the top of the head on each goat piece. Leave a tail of light tan yarn on 1 goat piece of each color for joining later.

15. Use 2 plies of black to work the long stitches and French knot eyes (1 wrap) on the goat pieces.

16. Use 2 plies of dark grey to work the long stitches and French knot eyes (1 wrap) on all sheep pieces. Work the face on two side 1 pieces and two side 2 pieces.

17. Assemble the sheep and goats as you did the pigs, using yarn to match each animal. Remember to use light tan yarn to join the goat horns.

18. Tack each animal to a base.

19. Cut out the remaining pieces on pages 33-37. Set the farm hand base aside.

20. Work the bases as you did the other bases.

21. Work the half cross stitches on all horse pieces.

22. Use 2 plies of yarn in the color indicated to work the long stitches, French knot eyes (3 wraps) and French knot nose (2 wraps) on the horse pieces.

23. Assemble the horses as you did the other animals using matching colors. Use black on mane and top of head on the brown horse and brown on the mane and head of medium tan horse.

24. Thread two 12" [30.5 cm] lengths of black yarn through the tail area (at the X's) on the brown horse. Adjust yarn to equal lengths on each side. Separate each strand into individual plies. Divide yarn into 3 groups (5 plies for each side and 6 for middle) and make a 1" [2.5 cm] braid. Tie a knot and trim ends about 1.5" [4 cm] below knot.

25. Use brown yarn to make the tail on the medium tan horse.

26. Tack each horse to a base.

27. Work the half cross stitches on all cow pieces.

28. Use 2 plies of color indicated to work the long stitches and the French knot eyes (3 wraps).

29. Assemble the cows as you did the other animals, using white up to the triangles and black between the triangles.

30. Use black to make tails (at the X's) as you did on the horses except cut to .75" [2 cm] below the knot.

31. Tack each cow to a base.

PEOPLE
1. Cut out and work the pieces shown on page 38. You may wish to leave an end of each color yarn as you work to be used for joining later because of the small pieces and color changes.

2. Work the farm hand base in light tan half cross stitch and overcast the edges.

3. Using 2 plies of brown, make a French knot eye (1 wrap) on the 2 farm hand and the 2 driver pieces.

4. Join each A arm piece to a matching B arm, using matching yarn.

5. Tack a light blue arm to each farm hand piece at the joining lines. Have hand towards the front.

6. Using matching yarn, join the farm hand pieces together. Join the face area first, then use 2 plies of brown to stitch the mouth (from side to side). Continue joining the 2 pieces adding small amounts of stuffing and stitching until all edges (except the bottom of pant legs) are joined.

7. Overcast the bottom of pant legs and tack the farm hand to the base.

8. Join the driver leg pieces together as you did with the arms.

9. Tack an arm and a leg to each driver piece at the joining lines. Have hands and feet facing forward.

10. Assemble the driver as you did the farm hand.

11. Overcast the long straight edge of each hat piece.

12. Join two hat pieces together along their unworked edges. Repeat to create a second hat.

13. Place the hats on the driver and the farm hand.

TRACTOR
1. Cut out all tractor pieces on pages 39-40.

2. Hold the tractor floor support piece under the tractor floor and work the black stitches through both pieces and overcast the black area only.

3. Work the half cross stitches on the rest of the tractor pieces.

4. Using 2 plies of medium grey, work the long stitches as indicated on tractor sides and front/top.

5. Join the tractor front/top piece to the side pieces, matching letters.

6. Join the knee wall from C to I and G to H.

7. Join these 4 pieces to the floor, working through both floor and support as if one piece (matching letters).

8. Join the seat piece to the upper and lower seat, matching letters.

9. Join these 3 pieces to the seat sides then to the tractor floor/support piece, matching letters.

10. Tack the driver to the seat and his shoes to the floor.

11. Using black, join the seat back to the seat sides, the upper seat and the tractor floor.

12. Overcast all edges of the steering wheel using black and tack it to the top edge of the knee wall.

13. Tack the driver's hands to the steering wheel.

14. Cut 4 outer rows off of 4 circles and work as shown on the chart (pg. 41) for front tires.

15. Place 2 front tires together (wrong sides facing) and overcast around edges to join together using black.

16. Work the stitches shown to make 4 back tires (pg. 41).

17. Cut and work the tire treads as shown on page 40.

18. Using black, join the short edges of each tire tread together to form a circle.

19. Join a back tire to each side edge of both tire treads.

20. Using black, tack the front tires to the tractor as indicated by joining lines.

21. Place the back tires on the tractor with the top of the tire 3 rows below the top of the seat and the front edge of tire at the edge of the driver's pant leg.

22. Tack the tires in place using black.

Layout Diagrams

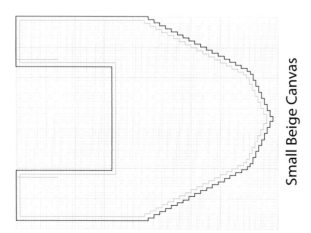

Small Beige Canvas

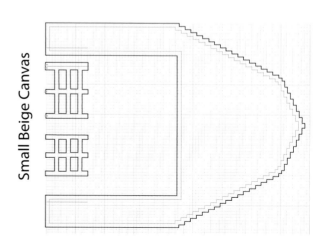

Small Beige Canvas

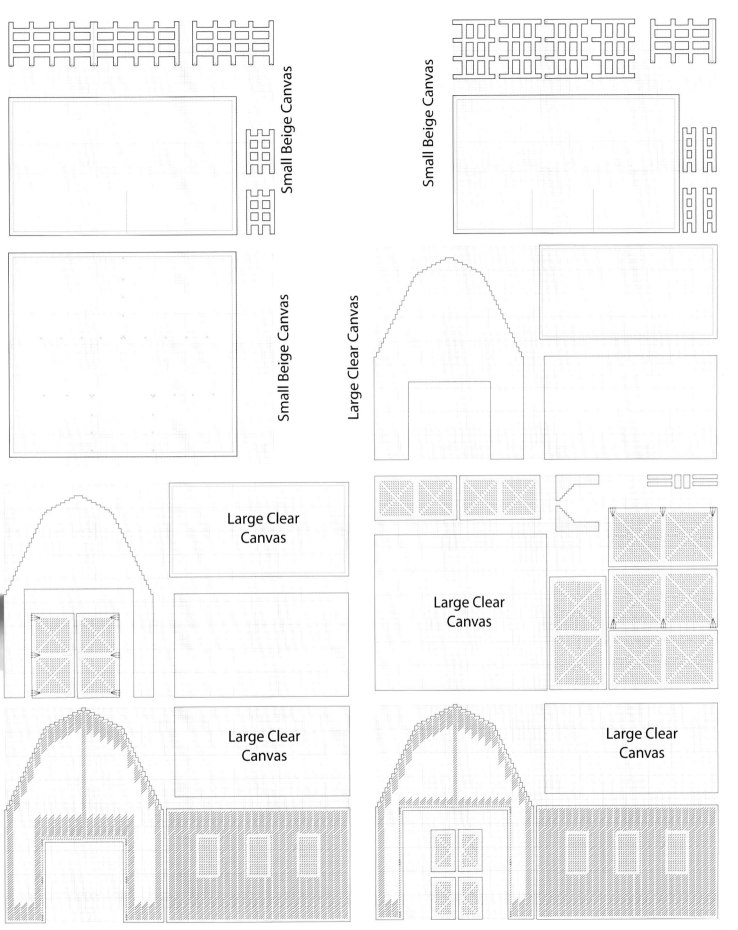

Small Beige Canvas

Small Beige Canvas

Small Beige Canvas

Large Clear Canvas

Large Clear Canvas

Large Clear Canvas

Large Clear Canvas

Large Clear Canvas

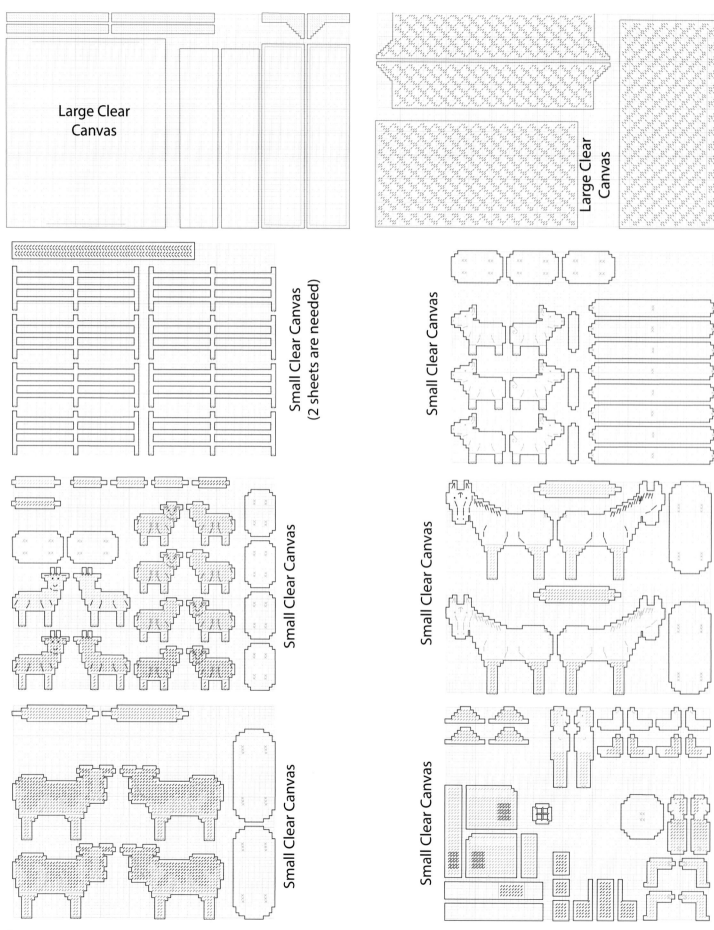

Large Clear Canvas

Large Clear Canvas

Small Clear Canvas
(2 sheets are needed)

Small Clear Canvas

Small Clear Canvas

Small Clear Canvas

Small Clear Canvas

Small Clear Canvas

Front Support (66 x 86 threads)
Large Clear Canvas

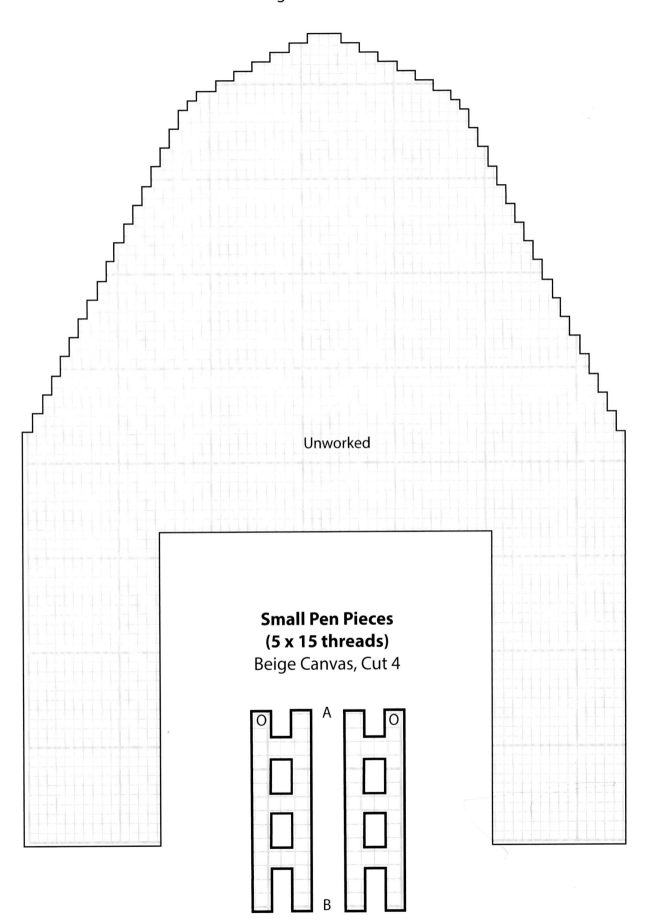

Unworked

**Small Pen Pieces
(5 x 15 threads)**
Beige Canvas, Cut 4

O   A   O

B

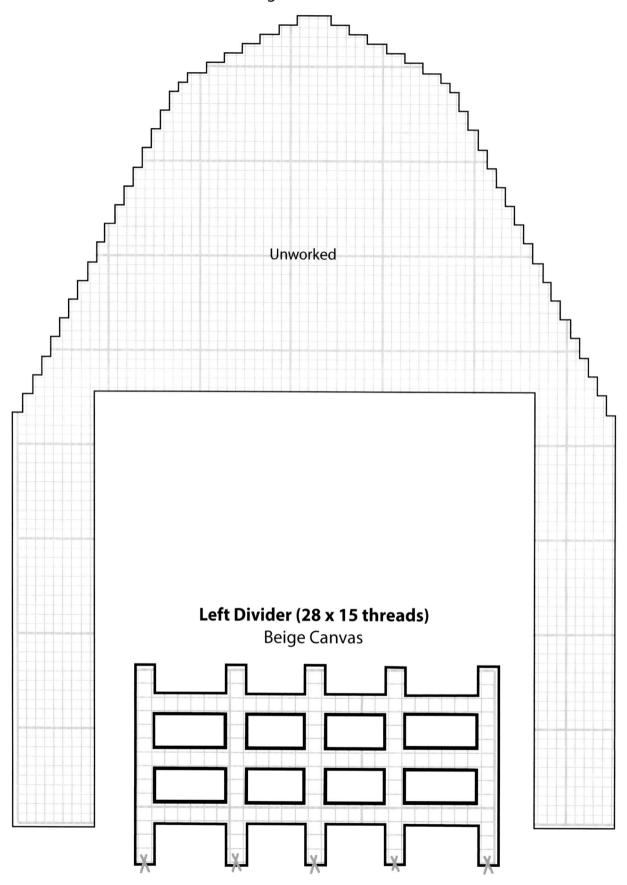

Back Support (66 x 86 threads)
Large Clear Canvas

Unworked

Left Divider (28 x 15 threads)
Beige Canvas

Side Support (76 x 44 threads)
Large Clear Canvas, Cut 2

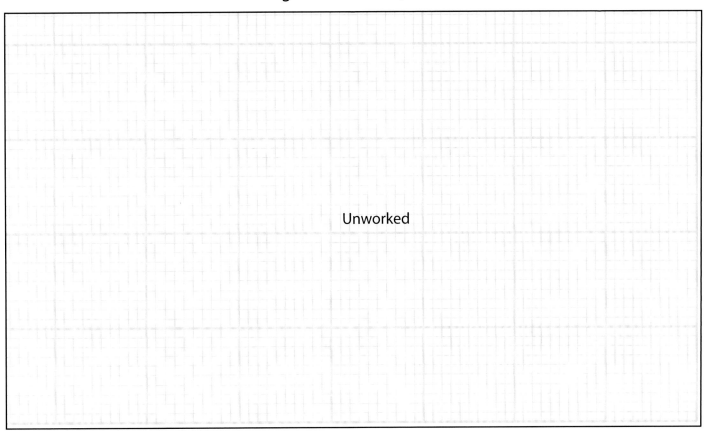

Unworked

Front Left Gate
(14 x 15 threads)
Beige Canvas

Back Right Gate
(20 x 15 threads)
Beige Canvas

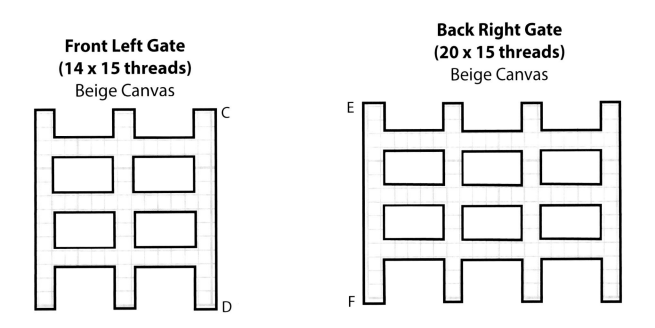

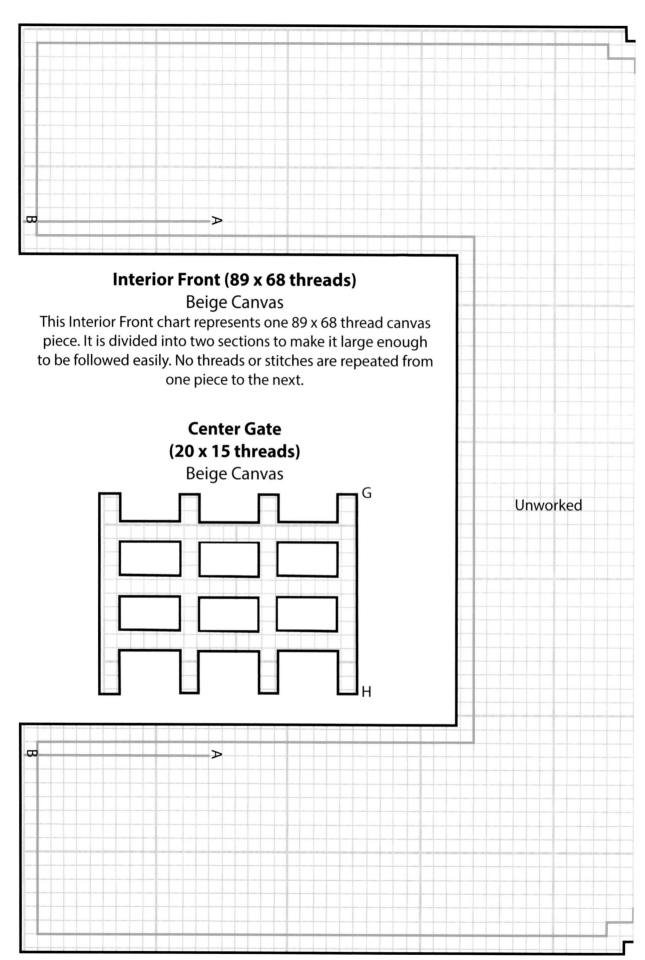

Interior Front (89 x 68 threads)
Beige Canvas
This Interior Front chart represents one 89 x 68 thread canvas piece. It is divided into two sections to make it large enough to be followed easily. No threads or stitches are repeated from one piece to the next.

**Center Gate
(20 x 15 threads)**
Beige Canvas

Unworked

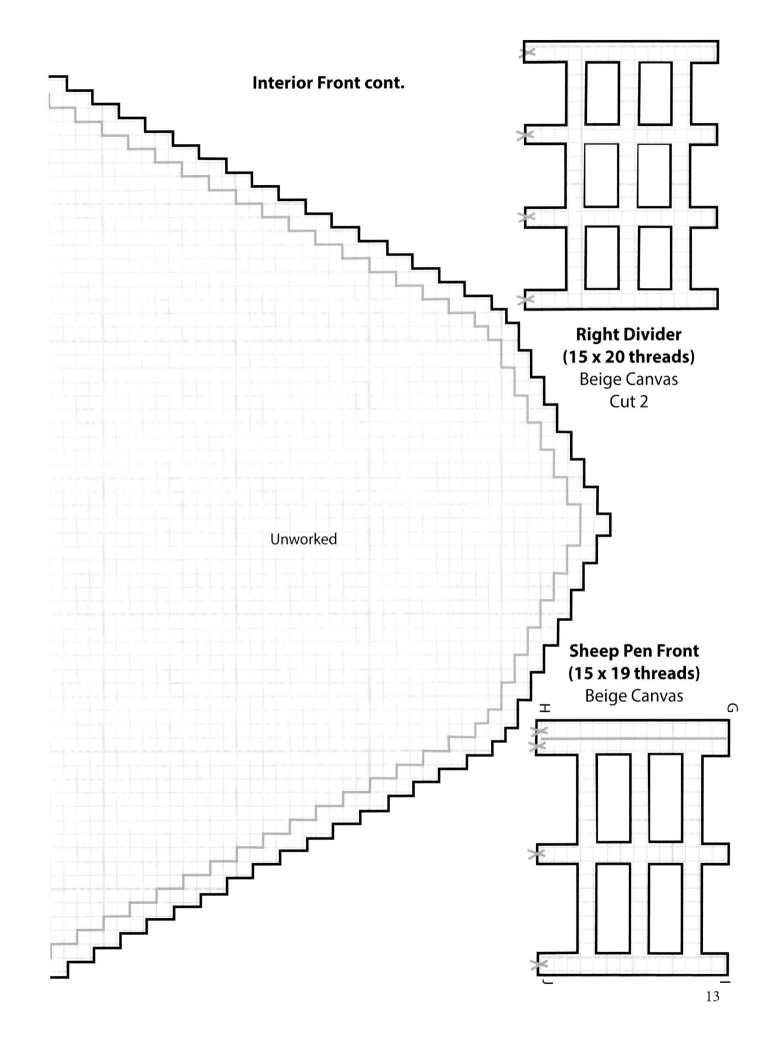

Interior Front cont.

Right Divider
(15 x 20 threads)
Beige Canvas
Cut 2

Unworked

Sheep Pen Front
(15 x 19 threads)
Beige Canvas

H

G

J

13

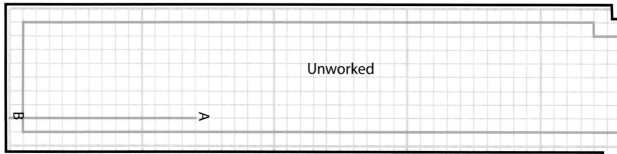

Unworked

Interior Back (89 x 68 threads)
Beige Canvas
This Interior Back chart represents one 89 x 68 thread canvas piece. It is divided into two sections to make it large enough to be followed easily. No threads or stitches are repeated from one piece to the next.

Pig Pen Front (23 x 15 threads)
Beige Canvas

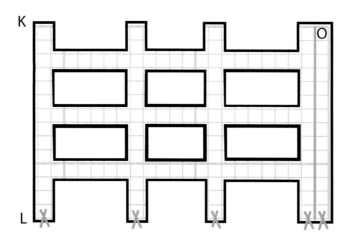

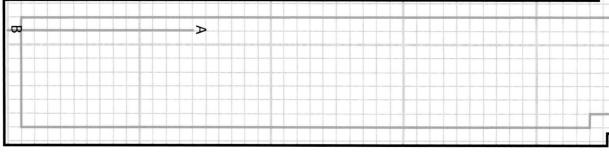

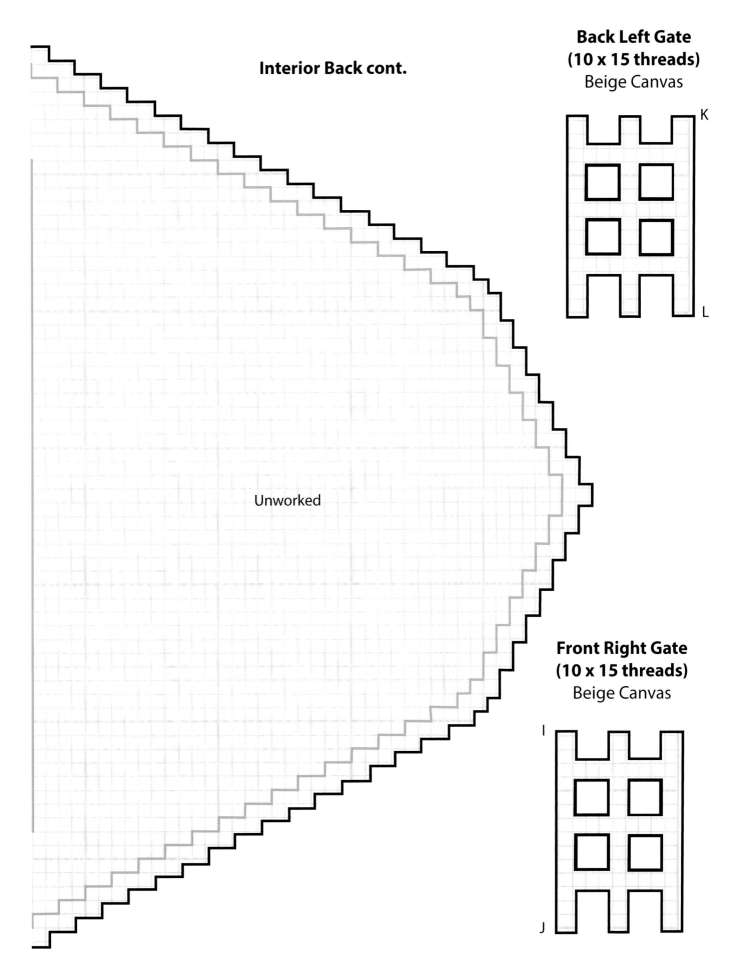

Interior Back cont.

Unworked

**Back Left Gate
(10 x 15 threads)**
Beige Canvas

K

L

**Front Right Gate
(10 x 15 threads)**
Beige Canvas

I

J

Right Interior Side (78 x 46 threads)
Beige Canvas

This Right Interior Side chart represents one 78 x 46 thread canvas piece. It is divided into two sections to make it large enough to be followed easily. No threads or stitches are repeated from one piece to the next.

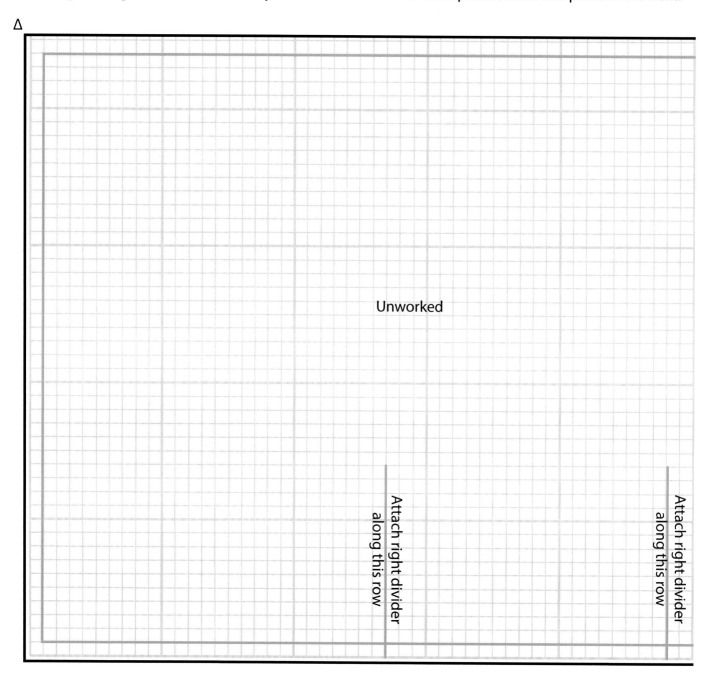

Unworked

Attach right divider along this row

Attach right divider along this row

Right Interior Side cont.

Δ

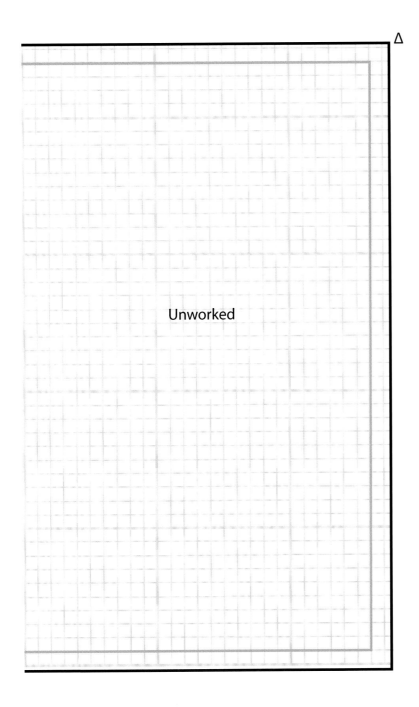

Unworked

Left Interior Side (78 x 46 threads)

Beige Canvas

This Left Interior Side chart represents one 78 x 46 thread canvas piece. It is divided into two sections to make it large enough to be followed easily. No threads or stitches are repeated from one piece to the next.

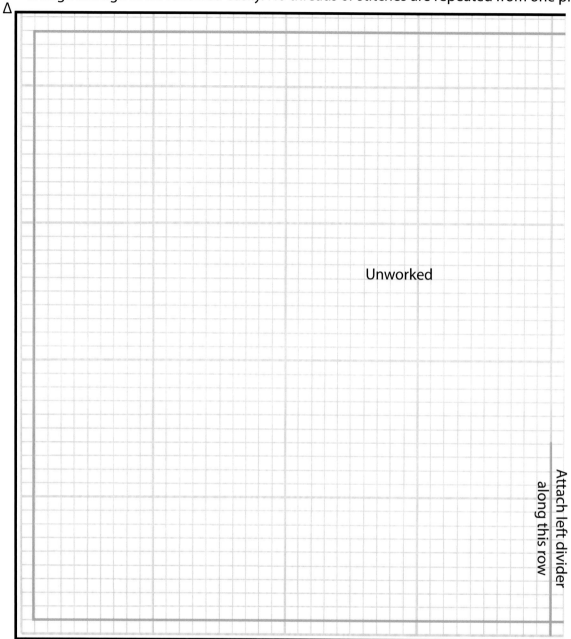

Unworked

Attach left divider along this row

Left Interior Side cont.

Long Pen Piece
(15 x 59 threads)
Beige Canvas

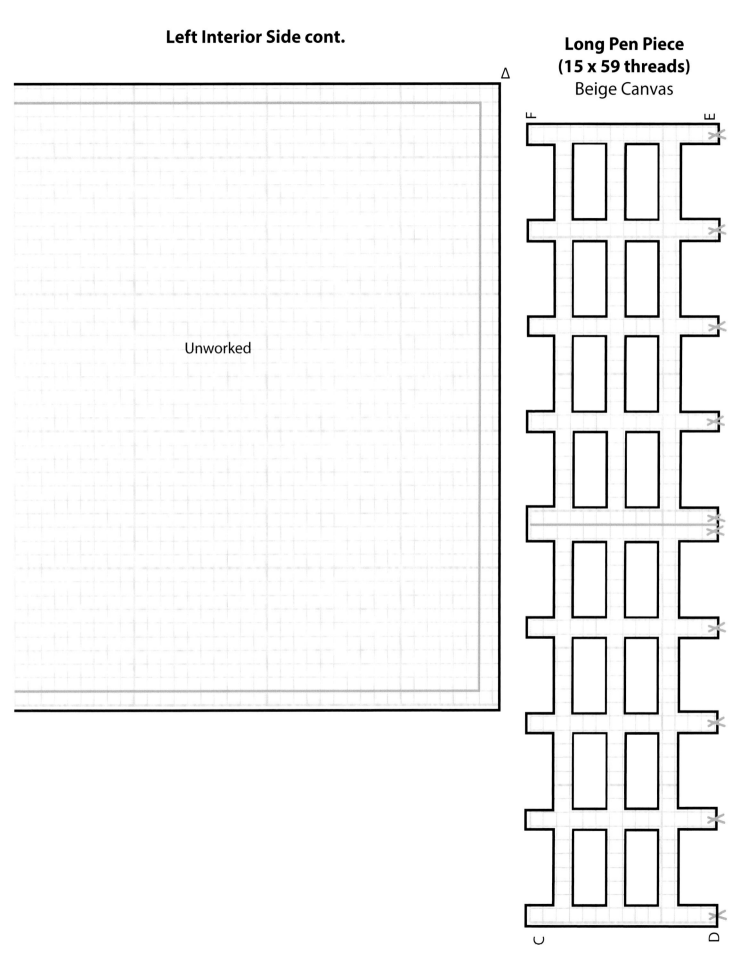

Unworked

Base Support (76 x 66 threads)
Large Clear Canvas

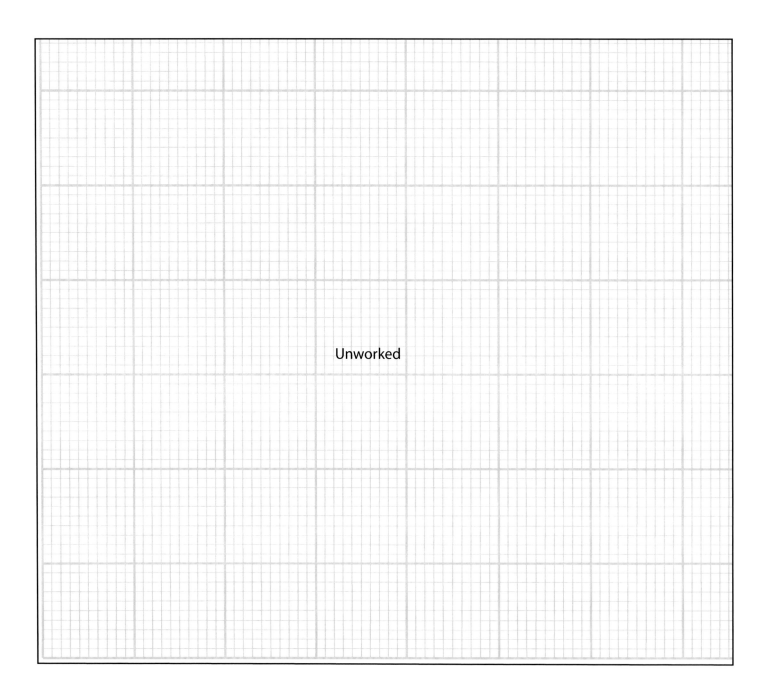

Unworked

Lower Roof Support (76 x 38 threads)
Large Clear Canvas, Cut 2

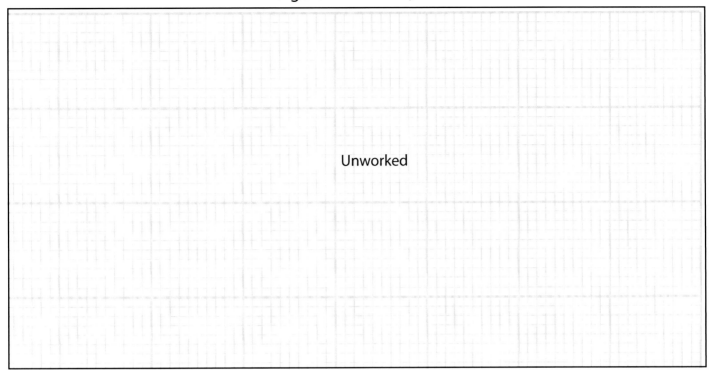

Unworked

Interior Lower Roof (78 x 40 threads)
Large Clear Canvas, Cut 2

A

B

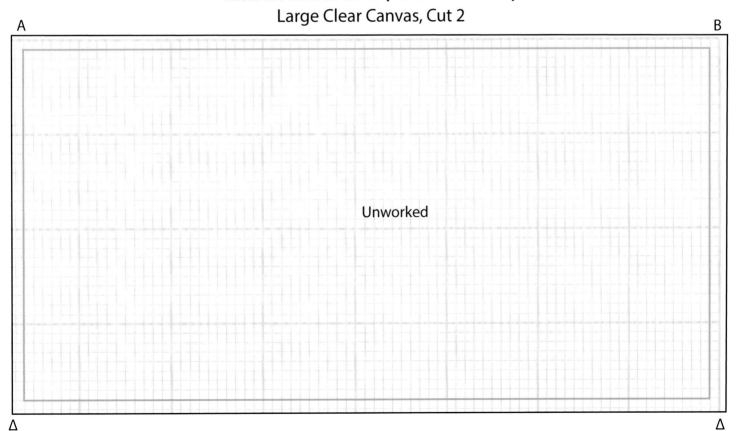

Unworked

Δ

Δ

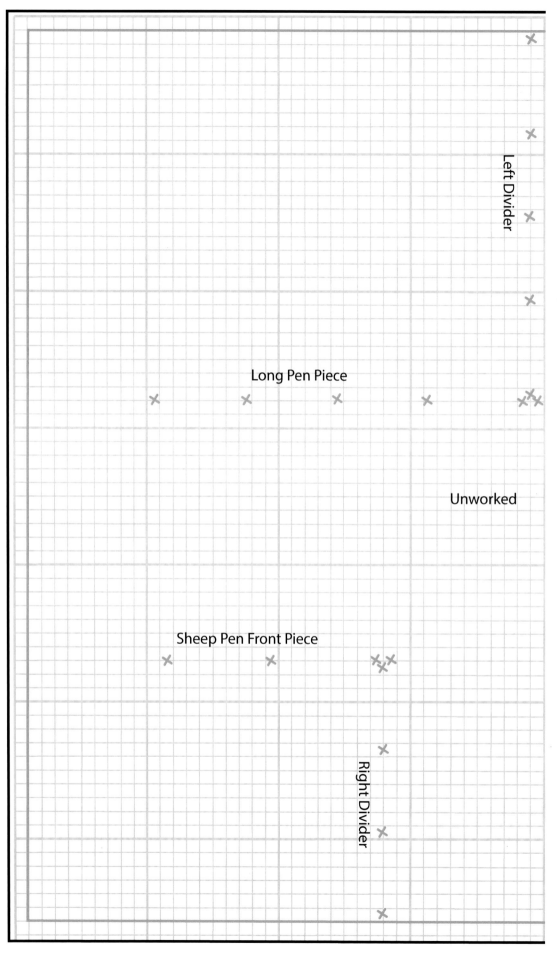

Interior Base (78 x 68 threads)
Beige Canvas
This Interior Base chart represents one 78 x 68 thread canvas piece. It is divided into two sections to make it large enough to be followed easily. No threads or stitches are repeated from one piece to the next.

Left Divider

Front Edge

Long Pen Piece

Unworked

Sheep Pen Front Piece

Right Divider

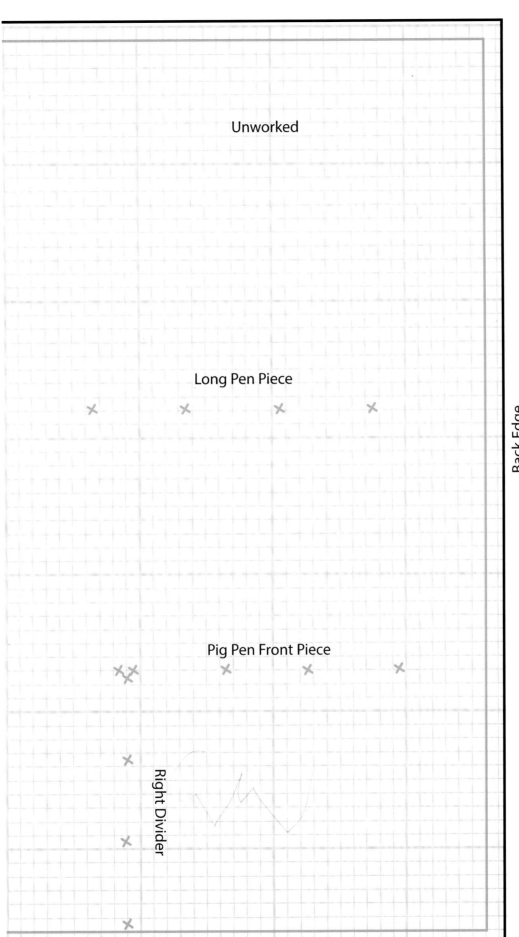

Unworked

Long Pen Piece

Pig Pen Front Piece

Right Divider

Back Edge

Top Roof Support
(17 x 76 threads)
Large Clear Canvas, Cut 2

Interior Top Roof Piece
(19 x 78 threads)
Large Clear Canvas, Cut 1 of each

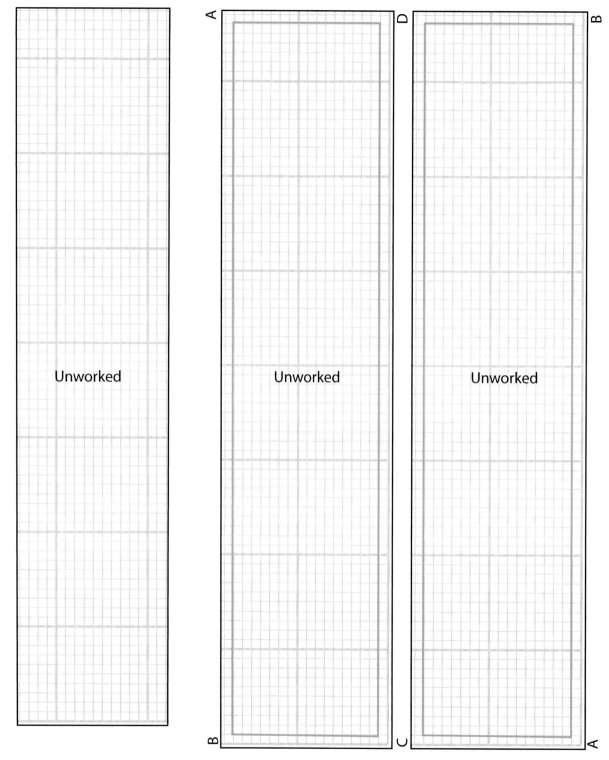

Unworked

Unworked

Unworked

Exterior Front (70 x 91 threads)
Large Clear Canvas

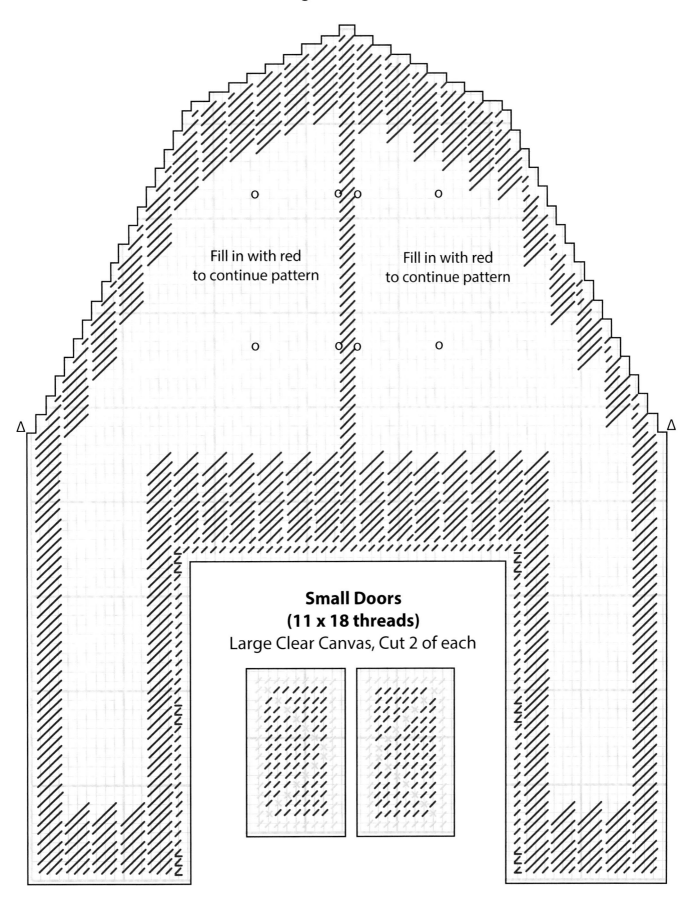

Fill in with red
to continue pattern

Fill in with red
to continue pattern

**Small Doors
(11 x 18 threads)**
Large Clear Canvas, Cut 2 of each

Exterior Back (70 x 91 threads)
Large Clear Canvas

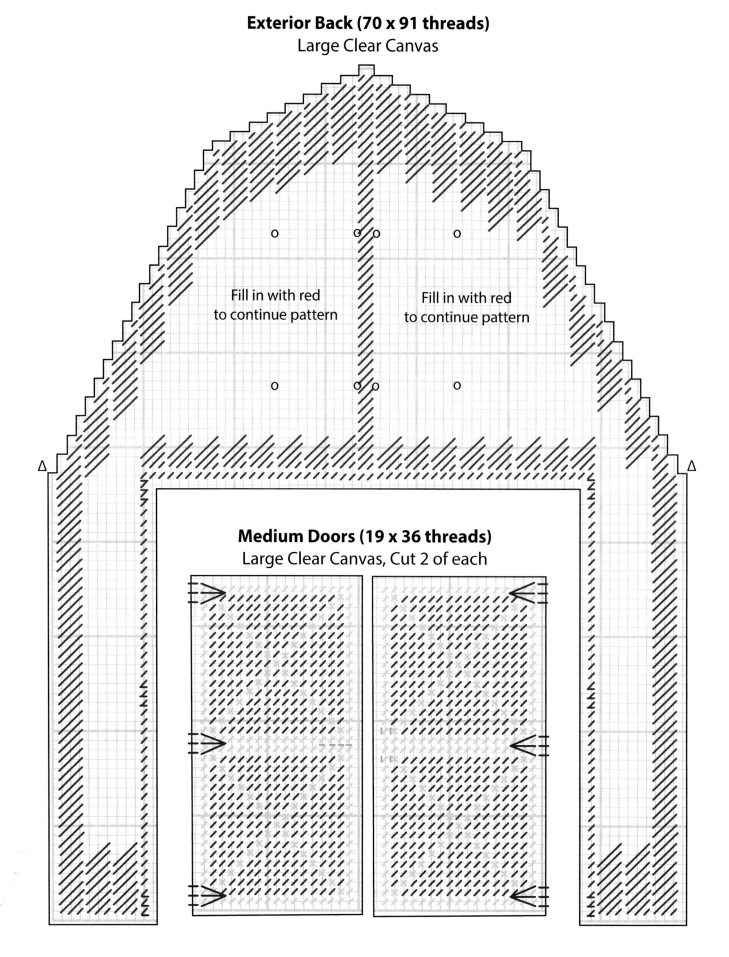

Fill in with red
to continue pattern

Fill in with red
to continue pattern

Medium Doors (19 x 36 threads)
Large Clear Canvas, Cut 2 of each

Exterior Side (48 x 80 threads)
Large Clear Canvas, Cut 2

Door Latch Pieces (11 x 2, 3 x 6, 11 x 2 threads)
Large Clear Canvas

Large Doors (25 x 48 threads)
Large Clear Canvas, Cut 2 of each

Lower Roof Trim Pieces (4 x 45 threads)
Large Clear Canvas, Cut 2 of each

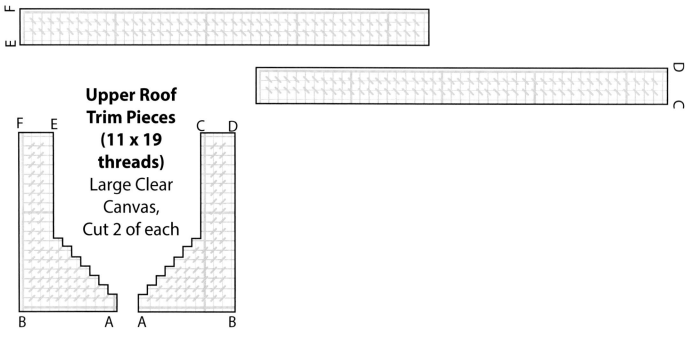

Upper Roof Trim Pieces (11 x 19 threads)
Large Clear Canvas, Cut 2 of each

Exterior Top Roof (20 x 102 threads)
Large Clear Canvas, Cut 2

Exterior Lower Roof (45 x 88 threads)
Large Clear Canvas, Cut 2

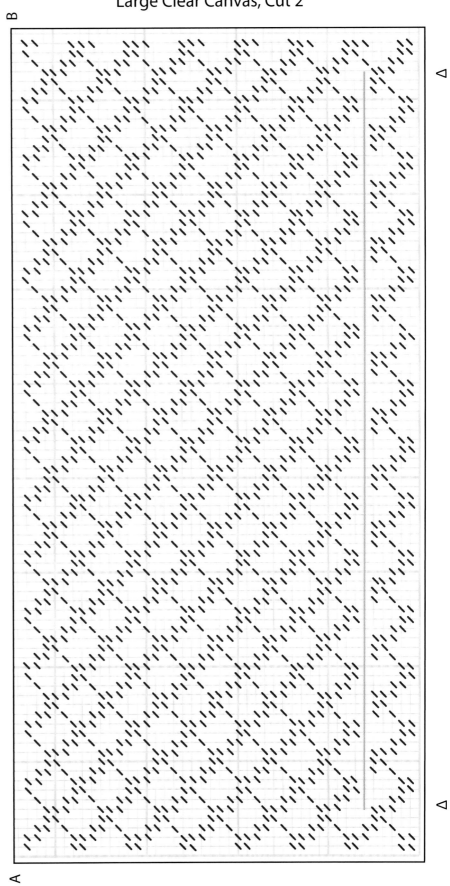

29

Exterior Base (70 x 80 threads)
Large Clear Canvas

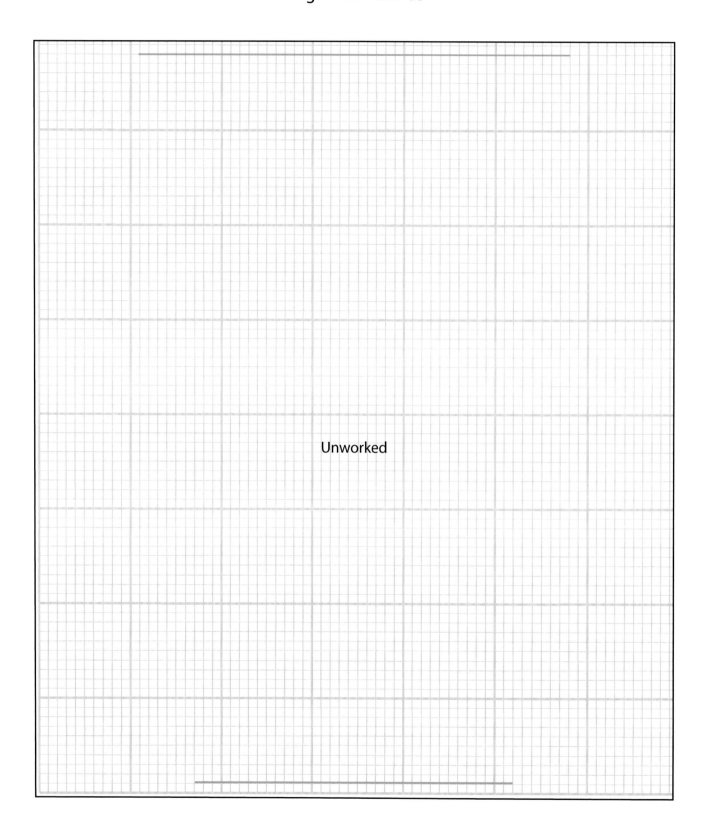

Unworked

Fence (44 x 15 threads)
Small Clear Canvas, Cut 16

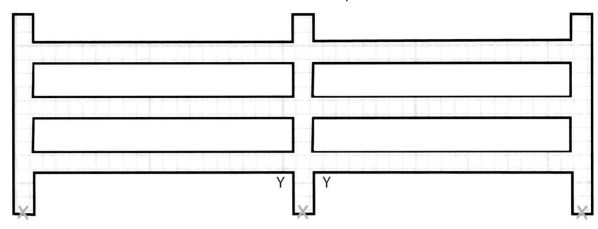

Fence Base (44 x 6 threads)
Small Clear Canvas, Cut 8

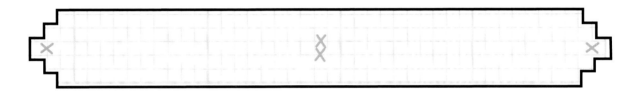

Pig Base (18 x 11 threads)
Small Clear Canvas, Cut 3

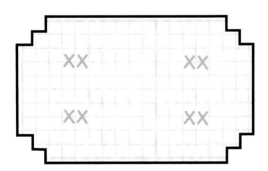

Pig Belly (14 x 4 threads)
Small Clear Canvas, Cut 3

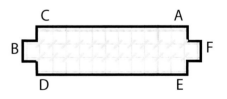

Pig Sides (19 x 17 threads)
Small Clear Canvas,
Cut 3 of each

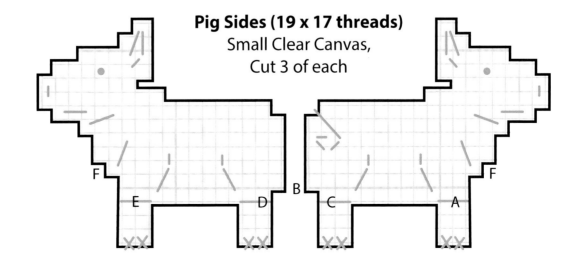

Side 1   **Side 2**

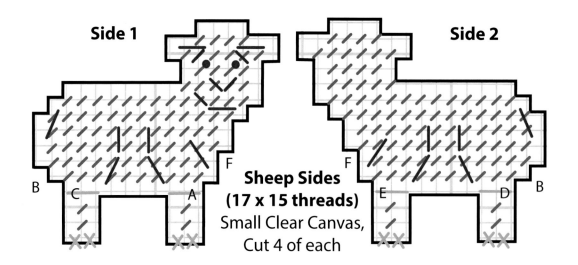

**Sheep Sides
(17 x 15 threads)**
Small Clear Canvas,
Cut 4 of each

Sheep Belly (13 x 4 threads)
Small Clear Canvas, Cut 4

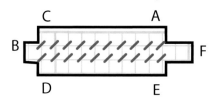

Sheep Base (16 x 11 threads)
Small Clear Canvas, Cut 4

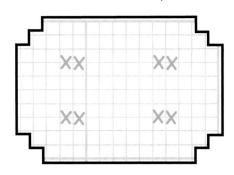

Goat Belly (17 x 4 threads)
Small Clear Canvas, Cut 2

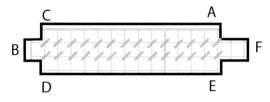

Goat Sides (20 x 20 threads)
Small Clear Canvas,
Cut 2 each

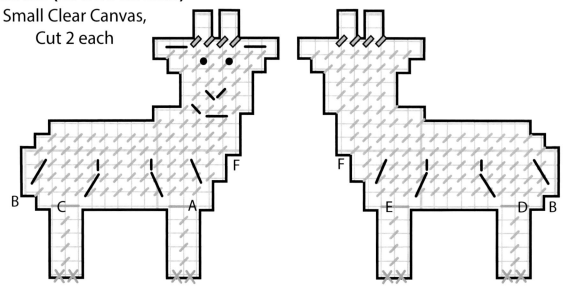

Goat Base (18 x 11 threads)
Small Clear Canvas, Cut 2

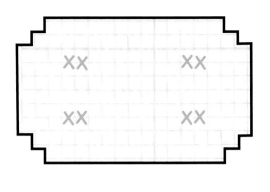

Horse A Base (31 x 15 threads)
Small Clear Canvas

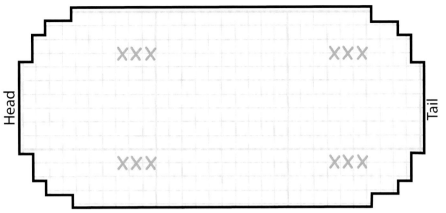

Horse A Belly (30 x 6 threads)
Small Clear Canvas

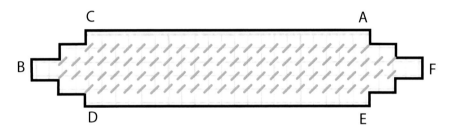

Horse A Front (37 x 33 threads)
Small Clear Canvas

Fill in with brown half cross stitch

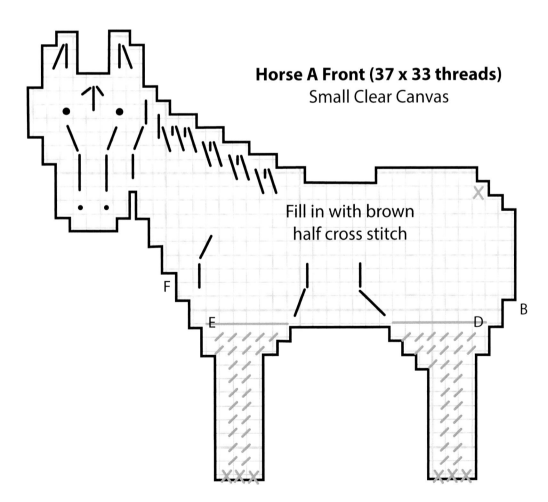

33

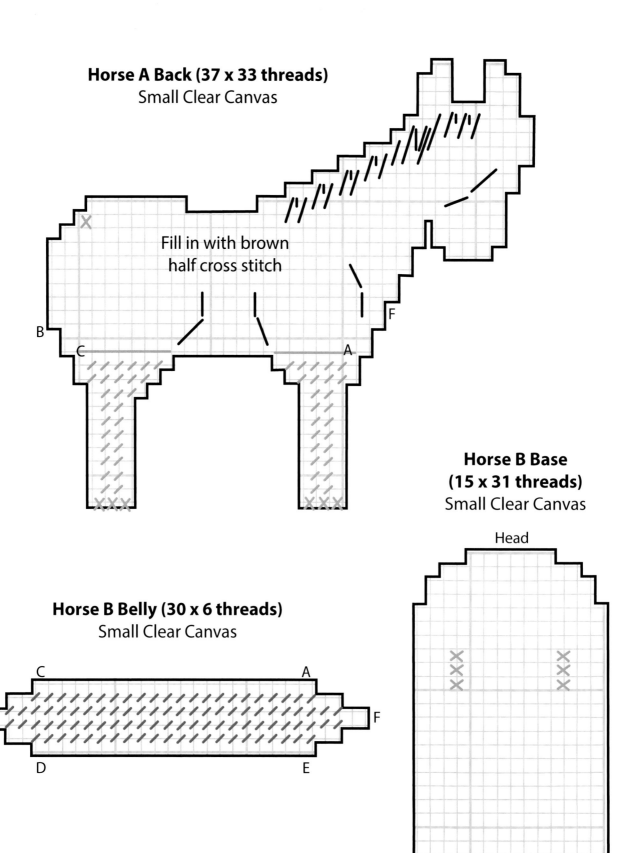

Horse A Back (37 x 33 threads)
Small Clear Canvas

Fill in with brown
half cross stitch

B

C   A

F

Horse B Belly (30 x 6 threads)
Small Clear Canvas

C   A

B   F

D   E

**Horse B Base
(15 x 31 threads)**
Small Clear Canvas

Head

Tail

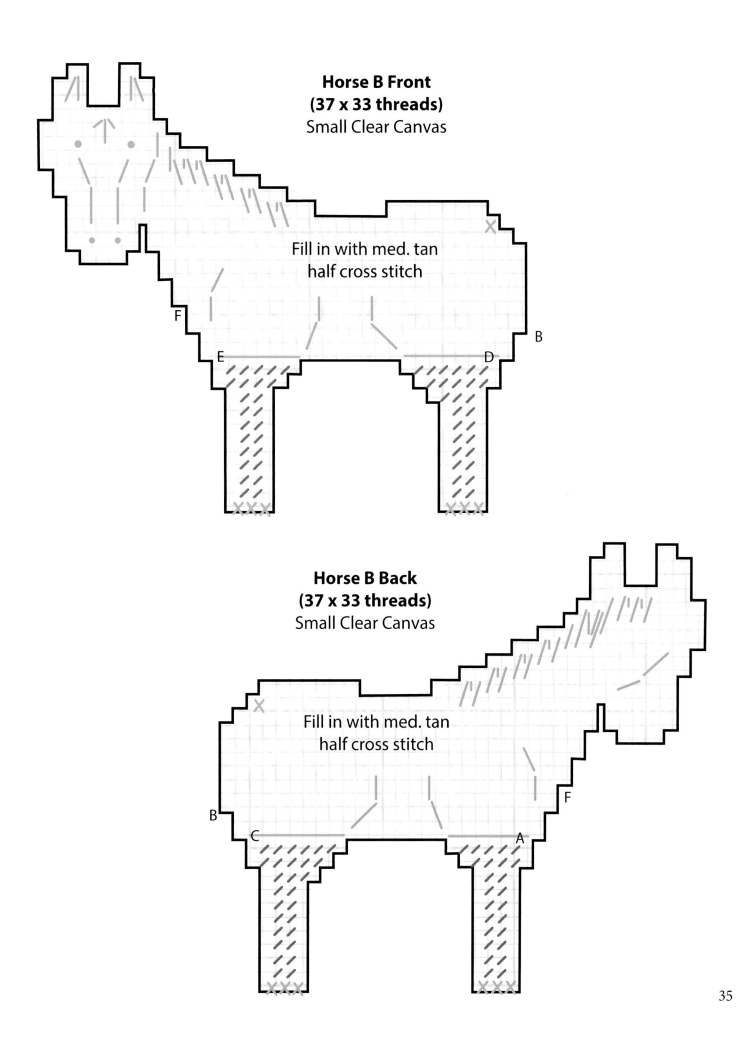

Horse B Front
(37 x 33 threads)
Small Clear Canvas

Fill in with med. tan
half cross stitch

Horse B Back
(37 x 33 threads)
Small Clear Canvas

Fill in with med. tan
half cross stitch

Cow A Front
(36 x 25 threads)
Small Clear Canvas

Cow Base
(15 x 31 threads)
Small Clear Canvas, Cut 2

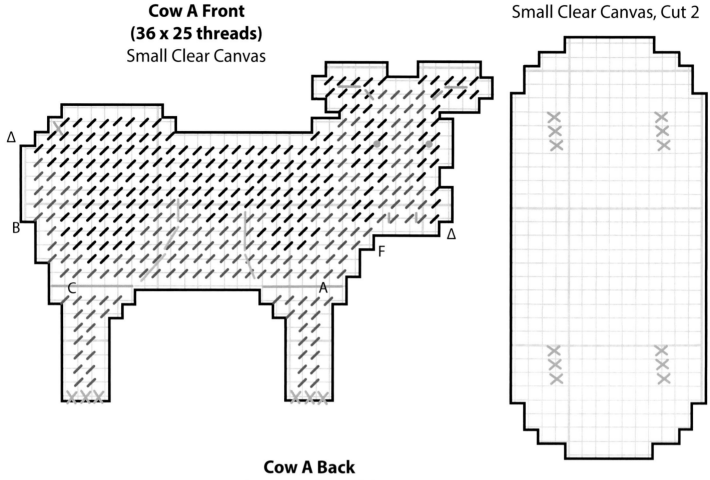

Cow A Back
(36 x 25 threads)
Small Clear Canvas

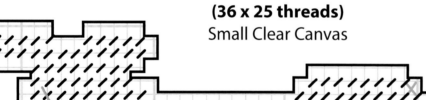

Cow Belly (30 x 6 threads)
Small Clear Canvas, Cut 2

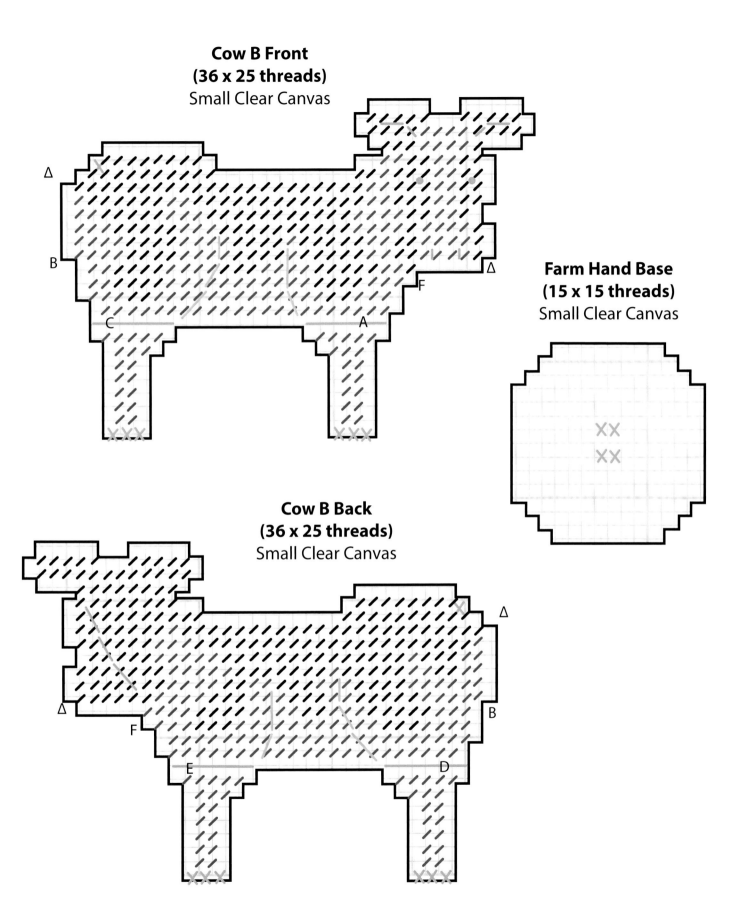

Cow B Front
(36 x 25 threads)
Small Clear Canvas

Farm Hand Base
(15 x 15 threads)
Small Clear Canvas

Cow B Back
(36 x 25 threads)
Small Clear Canvas

Farm Hand (7 x 27 threads)
Small Clear Canvas

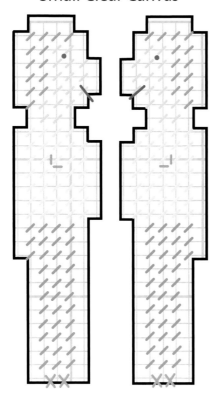

Driver (7 x 20 threads)
Small Clear Canvas

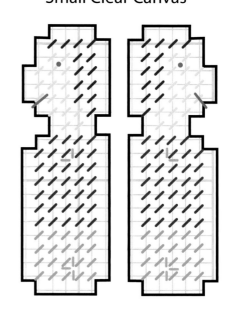

Farm Hand Arms (9 x 8 threads)
Small Clear Canvas, Cut 2 each

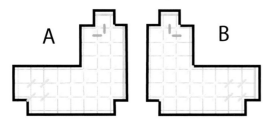

Driver Arms (9 x 8 threads)
Small Clear Canvas, Cut 2 each

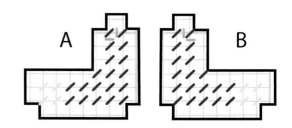

Legs (11 x 10 threads)
Small Clear Canvas, Cut 2 each

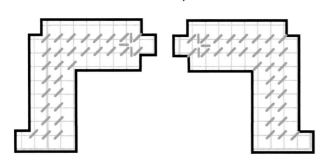

Hat (14 x 6 threads)
Small Clear Canvas, Cut 4

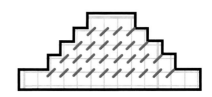

Tractor Floor Support (34 x 6 threads)
Small Clear Canvas

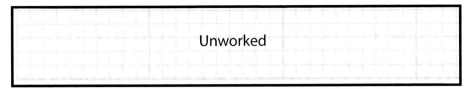

Unworked

Tractor Floor (34 x 6 threads)
Small Clear Canvas

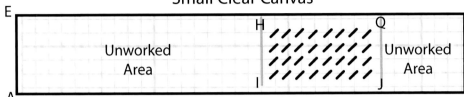

Unworked Area

Unworked Area

Tractor Front/Top
(6 x 31 threads)
Small Clear Canvas

Tractor Side
(18 x 15 threads)
Small Clear Canvas

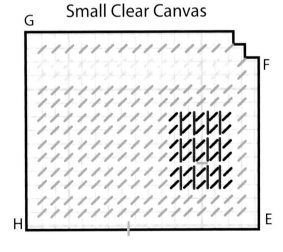

Tractor Side
(18 x 15 threads)
Small Clear Canvas

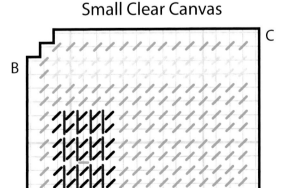

Steering Wheel
(7 x 7 threads)
Small Clear Canvas

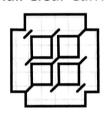

Knee Wall
(6 x 15 threads)
Small Clear Canvas

Upper Seat
(6 x 8 threads)
Small Clear Canvas

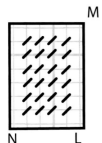

M

N L

Seat
(6 x 6 threads)
Small Clear Canvas

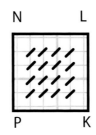

N L

P K

Tire Tread
(6 x 63 threads)
Small Clear Canvas,
Cut 2

Seat Side (7 x 14 threads)
Small Clear Canvas

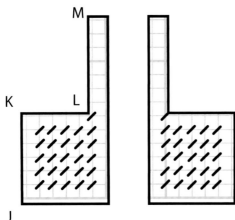

M

K L

J

Seat Back
(6 x 14 threads)
Small Clear Canvas

Lower Seat
(6 x 7 threads)
Small Clear Canvas

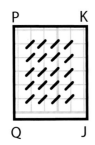

P K

Q J

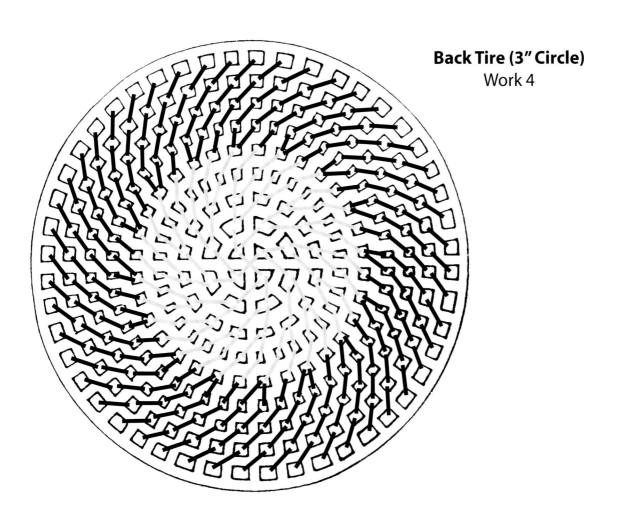

Back Tire (3" Circle)
Work 4

**Front Tire
(3" Circle)**
Cut and work 4

General Instructions

NOTE:
Please read all of the instructions before beginning. When joining pieces, refer to photos and notice whether right side of stitching should face in or out. You may need to use a few common household items to complete your project.

GENERAL INSTRUCTIONS:
Cutting the canvas must be done very carefully. If you miscut, the piece is ruined and you'll have to cut another piece. Our graphs show the shape of the pieces when they are cut out, making it easier for you to follow the cutting line. To cut, count bars, not holes. On each graph we show the total maximum number of bars required for each piece. (If you find it necessary to mark on canvas, use a pencil, but use it cautiously as the yarn will pick up the marks.) Plastic canvas is hand washable but do not put it in the dryer and do not dry clean. Cut in the space between the bars (as shown on the graph) rather than on a bar. After cutting, you will need to trim off all plastic nubs that remain to give your work a more finished look.

STITCHING INSTRUCTIONS:
Using 1 yard pieces of yarn, keep an even tension, making sure canvas is completely covered. However, too tight a tension will cause the canvas to curl. Work row across, first from left to right, then returning from right to left. To begin strand, draw needle though canvas until about 1/2" [1 cm] remains at back. Hold this end close to canvas and catch it in stitches on reverse side of work. To end each strand, put needle through to back and draw under a few stitches to secure. Trim yarn close to work. All joining rows and indicated areas are unworked.

Stitches

Half Cross Stitch

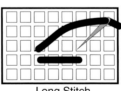
Long Stitch

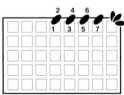
Overcast Stitch

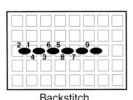
Backstitch

French Knot

Lazy Daisy

Notes